ANTHONY SANCHEZ

Edge of My Heart

From ICU to inspiration: A Dominican Son's Story

First published by AAF Publishing 2025

Copyright © 2025 by Anthony Sanchez

All rights reserved. No part of this publication may be reproduced, stored or transmitted in any form or by any means, electronic, mechanical, photocopying, recording, scanning, or otherwise without written permission from the publisher. It is illegal to copy this book, post it to a website, or distribute it by any other means without permission.

First edition

ISBN (paperback): 979-8-9996171-0-1
ISBN (hardcover): 979-8-9996171-1-8

Editing by Maria Allagianis
Editing by Meredith Long
Cover art by Anthony Sánchez

This book was professionally typeset on Reedsy. Find out more at reedsy.com

Dedication

*This book is dedicated to everyone who ever believed in me.
To anyone who thought they weren't good enough.
For those who gave up because life kicked the crap out of them
And they saw no way to make their dreams a reality.
This is for the ones who felt like they had nothing left to give.
"God is close to the brokenhearted." Psalm 34:18
He sees us, y'all.
Even when we think He doesn't—He sees us and He loves us.
A special dedication to my late dear friend and brother "Osh" (Woo!)
RIP*

Contents

Preface	ii
Acknowledgments	iv
Prologue	1
Chapter I: 2009	4
Chapter II: The dreams came next	10
Chapter III: The Bedlam on Eldert	23
Chapter IV: The Backyard Beyond	25
Chapter V: The Smell of Death	28
Chapter VI: What Covid Took	33
Chapter VII: The Doorway of Paradise… Forgiveness	36
Chapter VIII: Back to "reality"?	39
Chapter IX: Back from the Edge: Leg Raises and…	41
Chapter X: Post-ICU Hallucinations	44
Chapter XI: The Room with a View…	49
Chapter XII: "Ginger" The Red Nurse…	56
Chapter XIII: Requiem for the living	60
Chapter XIV: The Shift with Felix	66
Chapter XV: From Wreckage to Work	72
Epilogue	77
About the Author	80

Preface

People always ask me the same thing: "Did going through that make you appreciate life more?"
The truth? No. It didn't.
Because I already did.
I've always been that guy—the one who loved life. Who showed up. Who cracked jokes, played guitar, pulled a speaker out just to blast music while cooking for my family. I've always found joy in the little things, and I've always been grateful—for breath, for rhythm, for Brooklyn nights and Dominican mornings, for my kids' laughter echoing through the apartment.
Covid didn't teach me to value life—it taught me to stop wasting it.
Wasting it on relationships that drained me, on situations that gave nothing back. Wasted years I'll never get back—twenty to be exact—spent trying to prove myself. Trying to fix what couldn't be fixed and show up for people who wouldn't do the same for me or my family.
That's what changed. That's what the coma revealed.
Not just that I could've died—but that I had already been dying slowly, giving myself away piece by piece.
This book is about what happened when I stopped. When my body shut down and I slipped into a coma for three weeks during the height of the Covid pandemic. But more than that, it's about what woke up in me. The fire. The clarity. The refusal

to keep playing background music in someone else's life.

I was born in Bushwick, Brooklyn—raised in a world full of noise, soul, struggle, and love. Music saved me more than once. So did God. This story is rooted in both. It's about what happens when faith, rhythm, and purpose collide in the middle of crisis. It's about finding your voice again—sometimes with a mic, sometimes with a prayer.

There's a quote often attributed—though likely paraphrased—from the writings of Edmund Burke: "The only thing necessary for the triumph of evil is for good men to do nothing."

Whether or not he said it exactly that way, the message holds true. I've done enough nothing. That part of my life is over.

This is the story of what came next.

— Anthony Sánchez

Acknowledgments

I want to thank God for giving me life and for shaping the lens through which I see the world. I'll admit—my vision isn't always clear, and I don't always see things the way others do. But I see the world through a lens of love, and that love comes from my faith in Jesus Christ, the Son of God.

To my mother and father—thank you for being such powerful examples of integrity. You're not perfect, and you've never claimed to be, but your humility and your commitment to doing right have been a guiding light for me. I've never known either of you to intentionally hurt anyone. Your example has shaped the man I am today. Whenever my principles are tested and I find myself standing at a crossroads, it's your voices I hear in my heart—reminding me who I am. As a father now, I understand more than ever how hard it must've been. The fact that I still hear your guidance tells me I'll keep hearing it even when you're no longer here. That brings me peace. Because I know I'll never truly lose you—your lessons will stay with me long after your bodies are gone. I love you both deeply.

To my wife, Alejandra—you have been my anchor in storm after storm. You've always cheered me on, even when I doubted myself. We've walked through fire together, and I couldn't have asked for a better partner to share my life with. You're my "ride or die," and you've proved that more times than I can count. Thank you for never giving up on me.

And to all my friends and family from Bushwick—I rep you always. Everything I do is to make you proud. This Dominican kid from Eldert Street carries you with him in every word, every note, and every step forward. I love all y'all!

Prologue

April 9th — The Day the Dream Spoke Back

Before the ventilators. Before the coma. Before the classrooms and the mixing boards and having a family of my own.

There was a stoop.

Eldert Street — between Wilson and Knickerbocker Avenue in Bushwick, Brooklyn.

But not just any stoop.

This one belonged to my grandparents.

The steps were spotless. The sidewalk? Swept like clockwork. The windows? Crystal clear.

My grandfather, grandmother, uncles and aunts didn't just maintain the house — they honored it. Their work ethic wasn't quiet. It was LOUD. Consistent. Relentless. They cooked, cleaned, and held the home down with a kind of pride that you could feel as soon as you stepped onto the block.

That house was our headquarters.

We played skelly with bottle caps until our knees were filthy, sent punch ball shots flying into the next sewer cap, and dunked on each other using milk crates tied with twine to the fences or nailed to the top of someone's garage. We played football in the street, ran back inside for Nintendo marathons when it rained, then back out to play with our Transformers or G.I. Joe action figures or whatever cartoon had us locked in — Thundercats, Voltron— all of it.

Back then, I wasn't dreaming of music. I just wanted the latest action figure, maybe a new game cartridge, and enough daylight to get one more round in before dinner.

I could sing — always could — but I didn't see it as a calling. Not yet.

Then came the summer of '93 in Santo Domingo.

I was staying at my aunt's house, bored, flipping through her VHS tapes.

I found one — Phil Collins, live, performing "Against All Odds."

Him, a piano, the band and a spotlight.

Nobody handed me that tape. Nobody told me to watch it.

But I did. And it wrecked me in the best way.

It wasn't just a performance — it was a moment.

The kind that shakes you awake.

Right then and there, something shifted.

I want to do that.

Not just sing — I wanted to move people the way he moved me.

That was the day music became a dream.

Years later, I would come face-to-face with death.

Laid up in a hospital bed. Tubes in my throat. Floating somewhere between this life and the next.

But I came back.

And when I did, the words from a song I had written seven years earlier started echoing in my soul like a prophecy fulfilled:

"I'm running after my dreams — gonna run until I fall.

No more doubts left in me — breaking down every wall…"

I had released "Dreams" on April 9, 2013 —

not knowing that on April 9, 2020, I'd wake up from a coma, fighting for my life.

PROLOGUE

Same day. Seven years apart.
If you think that's a coincidence, you don't know my God.
Now, after everything, I find myself back on a different stoop.
Older. Slower. A few pounds heavier. Still dreaming but with a clear direction and focus.
This is where my story begins.
And this time, I'm not just dreaming for me —
I'm dreaming for my kids, my students, my brothers, and anyone who's ever felt like they wouldn't make it.
Welcome to my story.
Welcome to the edge of my heart.

Chapter 1: 2009

It was 2009—the year I decided to chase music while working full-time as a paraprofessional for the Department of Education. At that point, I had been married for four years to Alejandra (we tied the knot on July 23, 2005), raising my stepson, Felix. In 2007, we welcomed our daughter, Isabel, and man, she was beautiful. Holding her for the first time gave me a new understanding of God's love—if I could love my child this fiercely, how much greater was His love for us? Then in 2010, our second daughter, Analise, arrived, a complete surprise but just as much of a blessing. Life was moving fast, and it felt good.

With my wife's blessing—or so I thought (more on that later)—I threw myself into music. I started writing songs and formed a band with my boys: Hector "Conga" Rivera on percussion, William Steward on drums, Steven Duran on bass, and Piro Hernandez on keys. I was the lead singer and guitarist, and man, did I love those guys. They played for the love of music, and they played because they were my friends—guys I could count on. For five unforgettable years, we gave it everything we had. We were gigging almost every week, but the New York music scene wasn't kind to a guy like me. I struggled to get people to come to the shows—not even my own family showed up to support me.

CHAPTER 1: 2009

I have a massive family and this really hurt me for a long time. One uncle responded that it wasn't his scene. That I should play bachata instead so that I could make money. If I did that, then he would come to my shows. My response to him was, "But I'm your nephew. Why don't you just come and support me because you love me and you're my family? I don't play bachata because it doesn't really resonate with me, but if all of you guys show up, then it will be our scene because we would make it ours." Needless to say, he, nor anyone else in my family, ever really showed up. *(Except for that one time when Betty and my parents came to one of my shows in El Barrio in Harlem. That was special)*

I tried to ignore the hurt for a while, but it took a toll on me. I admit that I had no clue what I was doing. All I knew is that I loved to play music and perform live and I wanted to make a career of it. Unfortunately, I had no merchandise or physical products to give potential fans so the memory of what they heard was short lived and limited my traction. Eventually I reached out to some of my good friends in the music scene to see if they were willing to show love and give a brother a "friend's discount" on services, so that I could finally record an album. I'm blessed with some really great friends and because of their generosity, I was able to do just that. I began honing my craft in the studio and learned how to be a mixing engineer so that I could mix the album myself to save money. The process was so much fun and I learned a lot from my good friend Eli Menezes, co-producer on the record, who's always willing to share his wealth of knowledge with willing learners. Eventually, the album was released on all the available platforms and I started to play shows any and everywhere with my band mates Piro Hernandez, Steven Duran, Will "Bobo" Stewart, and Hector

"Conga" Rivera. We played at Wicked Willy's in the village, the Bitter End, Drom, Central Park, El Festival del Barrio, cafes, New York, New Jersey, you name it we tried it. Everyone that heard the music was impressed and really loved it, but I just didn't have the capital to promote or market myself as an artist. After five years of very little success, I gave it up (not completely) and went back to school to study Spanish and audio engineering at York College, paid for by the New York City Department of Education. One of the perks of being a paraprofessional is that they pay for six credits per semester, and I took advantage of that opportunity. It was not easy and it took me almost seven years to finish. Life, however, had other plans before letting me finish my degree, so it decided to throw a little screwball at me. On March 11th, 2020, I was sick with what I assumed and later confirmed was COVID, and I was deteriorating fast. The mayor closed the schools and shut the city down on March 15th, 2020, and I was home fighting for my life.

Being sick sucked, but what was even more frustrating was that I had just been accepted into the NYC Teaching Fellows *(a teacher's training program that is extremely accelerated and intense)* and had begun taking and passing all the necessary teaching certification tests, so I had momentum and traction and was well on my way to finally having a modicum of success. Which, for me, was apparently not in the cards, but I digress. Let's get back to the story. So while working full-time and going to school full-time, I was also playing small gigs as a guitarist and working as an Uber Eats delivery driver at night to earn extra money to make ends meet. I wasn't sleeping much between finishing school assignments and attempting to meet the needs of my wife and three children. This moment in my life was so exhausting, but I was hyper-focused on getting out of poverty

CHAPTER 1: 2009

and into a better financial situation because I was tired of not being able to give my family what they needed and sometimes what we wanted. As a man, not providing for your family is not an option because that's our duty; a duty that I felt I was failing at miserably. Remember when I said "or so I thought"? This was around the time that my wife and I began having some serious problems in our marriage that would lead to her distancing herself from me. This really broke my heart because I was still absolutely madly in love with my wife, and everything that I was doing at the time was for her and the kids. So, in addition to the mental and physical fatigue from work and school, there was the spiritual and emotional weariness from the conflict between my wife and I, and the combination of the two was taxing to say the least.

The thing about being a man is that no matter what's going on in your life, you've still got to keep pushing forward toward your goals. Despite the heartache and mental anguish, I kept checking off items from the TO-DO list given to all NYC Teaching Fellow candidates. One of those tasks was taking the GRE. It wasn't particularly meaningful—just something you had to do to say you did it—so I did it. I ended up scheduling it at a testing center in Long Island because it was the only place offering the exam within the next two weeks. While I was in the waiting room, I sat next to a woman who was ill. She was coughing next to me, and I didn't think anything of it. At this time, there were already reports going around about the COVID-19 outbreak in other parts of the world, but it wasn't really a thing in America yet. Anyway, I took the test, but I didn't even try. I think I just spelled ABACADABA all the way down on the multiple choice like in the movie "Who's the man?" with Ed Lover and Doctor Dre (hahaha) and left the building.

The GRE wasn't a vital test for what I needed, so I didn't put any effort into it.

A few days later, I began to feel fatigue and body aches. Then came the chills, then the fever, then the incessant coughing. I stayed locked away in my room and tried to do as the news reports were telling all young people infected with the virus: "stay indoors away from everyone"—it will pass, they said. Unfortunately for me, my body had been doing a lot of fighting up to that point, and it couldn't handle this new threat. I thought I was going to die. I had started to keep a log of how high my fevers were to keep records in case doctors asked me about them and by Wednesday, March 18th, my fever log was falling apart. Not because the fevers had stopped — but because I was fading. Only two entries that day. Not because I was getting better. But because I was losing the strength — and maybe the will — to keep tracking it. Felix, my oldest, was the first to really sound the alarm. He looked at me and saw the truth I was refusing to admit. "His lips are blue," he told my wife. "He needs to go to the hospital." But I was stubborn. Still convinced I could beat it at home. Still holding on to some false sense of control — like I had the power to manage this thing with Tylenol and sheer will. My wife, sick herself, tried to reason with me. But I wouldn't listen. I couldn't. I had already started slipping under. Then my mother came. Wrapped in layers like a mummy, covered from head to toe to protect herself from infection— she was scared but she came anyway. Walked into the fire to drag her son out.

She didn't ask.

She didn't plead.

She told me to get up.

And then told me to get dressed—like I was nine years old

CHAPTER 1: 2009

again. Her voice still carried that same weight of authority. Somehow, it made me move. And I did. That moment saved my life. And while I was being driven to the hospital — barely holding on — my kids were at home. On their own. No parents around, because my wife had to quarantine too. She was starting to show signs of a COVID infection. No certainty. Just a brother and two sisters...learning how to survive. Felix was 24. Isabel was 13. Analise was 9. They cooked for each other. Checked on each other. Held the house down while the world around them unraveled. I wasn't there. But they made me so proud. Because in the absence of their parents... they became each other's keepers. Eventually, my mother got me to New York Presbyterian Hospital in Queens. After a stress test showed my oxygen levels were dangerously low, I was admitted on March 19th, 2020. On March 21st, I was intubated and placed into a coma.

Chapter II: The dreams came next

Some were terrifying, some were funny, and others were beautiful, but in all of them, I was sick. The first dream I remember was surreal—somehow, I was in Tijuana, Mexico, with a 'Coyote' (not the animal, but a smuggler) trying to get me into the United States for medical care. I had no reason to need a smuggler—I was a U.S. citizen—but in this world, I did. I was lying in the back of his truck, hooked up to catheters at both ends, on a bed made of waste containers collecting everything my body expelled. As we approached the border, we were stopped by patrol guards who called over a lieutenant. The guards inspected the truck, suspecting drugs, and decided to break open one of the waste containers. The stench filled the air, and one guard gagged, shouting, "¡Teniente, es pura mierda que está saliendo de aquí!" (Lieutenant! there's shit coming out of these containers!) The lieutenant, equally disgusted, ordered them to patch it up and let us pass. Before leaving, I managed to grab a pen and paper and write a sincere thank-you note to the lieutenant, genuinely grateful that he had allowed us to pass. I carefully chose my words, expressing my appreciation in Spanish and including a Dominican colloquialism as a way to add a touch of my culture to the note. However, when the lieutenant read it, he chuckled and began to mock my phrasing,

CHAPTER II: THE DREAMS CAME NEXT

twisting my words into a joke among his men. Annoyed and insulted, I penned a rebuttal, carefully phrasing it with linguistic precision. Though I couldn't remember the exact words I used in the dream, I knew they were eloquent, sharp, and deliberate. What I do recall is the essence of what I was trying to communicate—that language is rich, varied, and deeply tied to culture. I ended with, "Con todo el respeto para usted y su oficina, en España se dice así, se escribe así, y se pronuncia de esta manera, pero en buen dominicano se dice así... hijo 'e puta!" (*English Translation: "With all due respect to you and your office, in Spain it's said like this, written like this, and pronounced like this, but in good Dominican it's said like this... you s.o.b!*) The lieutenant's smugness faded, and without another word, we were waved through. Then, we were on our way to Detroit, where my coyote friend dropped me off at a hospital in the middle of a gang war—de Guatemala a guatapeor.

From there, my reality kept shifting, merging conflict, survival, and deep personal wounds...

In the next dream I found myself being honored for my service as a police officer, receiving an award and an honorary bachelor's degree. There was a parade, but I was hesitant to be publicly associated with a particular political leader. I had been playing both sides—gathering information on both the corrupt official, and the gang leaders. Unfortunately, my attempts at remaining neutral failed when the political leader ensured I was seen with her on live TV. The gangs viewed me as a snitch and placed a bounty on my head.

Not long after, I was ambushed. While driving through the Bronx, I was shot, my car flipping over from the impact. As I lay trapped in the wreckage, the shooter approached to finish the job, but before he could, my cousins and their crew arrived, saving me. They called the police, and soon, a shootout erupted around me. My cousins shielded me with a thick metal plate, extracting me from the chaos and transporting me to a hospital.

My reality shifted again. I was in a hospital, but my estranged wife had set me up for a televised "gotcha" moment, making it seem like I was faking my illness and had been unfaithful. I was humiliated, broken, and alone—until my mother and younger brother appeared, trying to comfort me.

But I wasn't safe. The hospital itself was being dismantled—walls breaking apart like a jigsaw puzzle. My mother, unsuspecting of what was happening, stepped out of the bathroom as she finished her nightly routine. Just as she was about to exit, she nearly stepped forward into empty space—what had been a solid floor was now gone. We had been on the fourth floor, but now she was teetering on the edge of a sheer drop to the ground level. At the last second, she caught herself, her face twisting in shock and terror.

From her perspective, the scene was one of pure chaos. The floors, walls, and ceilings remained intact and sturdy, but they were coming apart like pieces of a puzzle, shifting and separating, leaving massive, gaping voids between them. These gaps were not just obstacles; they were deadly. Anyone who miscalculated a step or failed to recognize the shifting layout could easily fall through and perish. My hospital bed, once securely positioned, was now on a section of flooring that had drifted away, suspended over an open abyss. My brother's cot, which had been against the far wall, was now disconnected from any solid foundation, hovering three feet away from me. The once-cohesive hospital room was now fragmented, transformed into a treacherous maze where every movement carried the risk of falling into nothingness.

CHAPTER II: THE DREAMS CAME NEXT

She gritted her teeth, steadying herself, and scanned for a way to move without plummeting downwards. The weight of responsibility hit her all at once—she needed to act fast. Her first instinct was to retrieve her clothes and wake up my brother, who was still blissfully asleep, unaware of the disaster unfolding around him. Pressing herself against the remaining walls, she carefully moved along the edge, her heart pounding. Every step felt uncertain, the floor shifting beneath her as if it could crumble at any moment. She was like a ninja, moving with calculated precision through the dangerous terrain, determined to reach her son and make sure he was safe.

Eventually, she made it. She grabbed her clothes and reached my brother, shaking him awake and pulling him into the horrifying reality that had swallowed us whole. As my brother's eyes adjusted to the madness around him, my mother turned her attention to the figure overseeing the dismantling of the mock hospital suite. Her fear transformed into fury, and she stormed toward them, her voice sharp with anger. She demanded immediate transportation for me to a real medical facility, refusing to accept whatever was happening as anything other than an outrage. Meanwhile, my brother remained by my side, his stance firm, as if preparing for whatever might happen next.

And I believe this is when they moved me in the real world—from NY Presbyterian to Cornell, then to HSS in Manhattan. My mind, however, was still lost in the dream world, unaware that I was truly fighting for my life.

Then...

From there, my reality shifted back into the world where I was a police officer. The political official who had used me as a pawn had now set me up to take the fall, and I was being transported to prison. But this wasn't a typical prison—it was more like a local city lockup, housing prisoners from all walks of life. Because I was now a disgraced officer, I was placed among the general population, still bedridden and connected to catheters that collected my waste.

Lying there, I kept asking myself—how did I get here? How did I go from hero to criminal? How could she get away with this? I reached for my phone and called my union representative, hoping for support. But his voice was cold. He told me that he could no longer represent me, that I had brought shame to the shield, and that I was on my own.

As I processed this betrayal, the environment around me shifted again. What had been a prison now also became a bank—on one end of the same building, people were cashing checks and making transactions. The contradiction was jarring—how could a prison and a bank occupy the same space? Even in my subconscious, I was questioning the logic of the dream.

Before I could make sense of it, the room suddenly split. The second half of the space folded downward, creating a sharp 90-degree angle, like a broken bridge. As the structure shifted, a hardened criminal took the opportunity to seize control. He held hostages and declared that he was there to kill me—to finish what had been started back in the Bronx. But I couldn't move. I was bedridden, my body still weak, still tethered to the medical equipment.

He didn't believe me. He threatened to kill the hostages unless I proved that I was truly incapable of resisting. I assured him I wasn't lying and told him that if he wanted me, he would have to come get me—but only if he let the hostages go.

A frail prisoner beside me, barely more than a whisper of a man, spoke up. In a soft, docile voice, he confirmed to the

CHAPTER II: THE DREAMS CAME NEXT

assailant that I was telling the truth—that I was connected to an array of different machines and containers. The assailant considered his words, then barked an order—I had to remove my catheters myself.

I obeyed. The moment I did, waste spilled everywhere—drenching my bed, the sheets, the floor beneath me, and cascading down the newly formed 90-degree angle. The stench filled the air, sickening and inescapable. The assailant, determined to get to me, had no choice but to crawl through the mess he had forced me to create. The closer he got, the more disgusted he became. By the time he reached me, he was gagging, his bravado slipping.

He looked down at me, shaking his head. "I'm going to cover you in this sheet for about a minute," he said. "If you survive this, I'll let you go."

He yanked the soiled sheet over my face, suffocating me with my own filth. It wasn't just a test—it was torture, a twisted form of waterboarding, only instead of water, I was drowning in my own fluids. My lungs burned, my body writhed, every instinct screaming for air. But I survived.

I believe this moment mirrored a real-world struggle—one of the nights when my oxygen levels were plummeting, when the nurses and doctors were fighting desperately to keep me breathing. My body was failing, my lungs collapsing under the weight of the virus, but thanks to the prayers of my family and friends and the relentless efforts of the medical team, I made it through that terrifying night—both in the dream world and in reality.

From there, my reality shifted back to Detroit. This time, I wasn't completely sick, but I was getting worse. I had a friend who was a wealthy drug dealer, living a lavish lifestyle, and because of our friendship, I benefited from his success without being directly involved in his business. In this reality, I had a girlfriend—someone I don't recognize from my real life—but she was beautiful, and we shared in the luxury together.

We lived in a massive, well-furnished house with everything anyone could want—except for genuine love. As my illness worsened, I began to notice a shift. The woman I thought loved me became distant, impatient, annoyed at the burden of caring for me. My friend, however, never wavered. He made it clear to everyone that I was to be looked after at all times. But when he was away handling business, I took a turn for the worse.

I needed to get to a hospital, but my girlfriend refused to take me all the way. Instead, she planned to abandon me by the roadside, leaving me exposed to the brutal Detroit winter—accelerating my death. She was done with me, unwilling to deal with my decline. What she didn't know was that my friend had been monitoring her actions. Before she could carry out her plan, he intervened. He killed her on the spot.

Without hesitation, he loaded me into his car and drove me to the hospital himself, but what awaited me there was yet another conflict—another test of survival in this fractured reality.

As my friend pulled up to the hospital, it looked like a place where I would receive the best possible medical care. He knew this might be the last time we ever saw each other. Before they wheeled me inside, he hugged me tightly, telling me to keep fighting, to keep my head up. I reassured him—I wasn't going to quit. Then, they took me into a room and connected me to a ventilator. Up until this point, none of my dreams had placed me on life support, but now, I was. I believe this was the moment, March 21st, 2020, in the real world when they intubated me. The fractured reality—the shifting back and forth

CHAPTER II: THE DREAMS CAME NEXT

between different worlds—was, I think, my oxygen-deprived mind trying to make sense of what was happening, but failing miserably.

While I was in that hospital room, a shootout erupted between two rival gangs, and my room was caught in the crossfire. Twenty-two bullets shattered my window and struck me in the back. Fortunately, they were from small-caliber weapons, so the damage wasn't deadly—or at least, that was the reality my mind created to keep itself going. The doctors were too afraid to move me; they didn't want to risk being hit by stray bullets. It was a tense standoff—until a badass Mexican nurse stormed into the room, completely unfazed. She was calm, cool, and collected as she grabbed my hospital bed and rolled me out without hesitation. As she wheeled me into safety, she made a sharp remark about the doctor's lack of cojones and how he had failed to do what needed to be done to protect his patient.

Once I was in a new room, things didn't get any better. Two nurses with bright blue hair, identical twins, took over my care. They were the meanest nurses in the hospital, and their reputation preceded them. They were affiliated with one of the rival gangs in the east, and they carried themselves with the arrogance and power of that connection. While attending to me, they began lowering my oxygen levels, watching as I struggled for air. I couldn't breathe. My body panicked, but they only laughed, mocking me as they continued to suffocate me, turning down the oxygen little by little.

Then, the Mexican nurse returned. She didn't hesitate. She grabbed both of them by their hair and beat the living daylights out of them, dragging them out of my room and humiliating them in front of the entire hospital. One of the twins, humiliated and enraged, stormed off to her locker, retrieving a gun. She stepped into the middle of the hallway, intent on killing the Mexican nurse in retaliation.

But she didn't realize—the Mexican nurse was strapped too.

Before the blue-haired nurse could fire, the Mexican nurse pulled out her own gun and shot twice, killing her instantly. The other twin stood frozen, looming over her sister's body, unable to process what had just happened. Officers soon arrived, arresting the surviving twin for patient abuse and removing the body from the hallway.

With the chaos settled, the Mexican nurse came back into my room and adjusted my oxygen levels, allowing me to breathe again.

I believe this was one of the nights when my O2 saturation dropped dangerously low in reality. Later, after I woke up at the Hospital for Special Surgery, one of the nurses told me they had been trying to wean me off the ventilator to see if I could breathe on my own. My body fought that process, just as it had in the dream. But, once again, I made it through—both in the dream and in reality.

The chaos had died down.

I was still in Detroit, lying in that hospital room, now stable—at least for the moment. The gang war outside had faded, the bullets stopped flying, and for the first time, things felt... still.

That's when the visitors started showing up.

First, Pastor Danny Torres and Josh Ramos—two friends of mine who had traveled all the way from New York just to see me. They came with my son, who looked concerned but strong. He wanted to make sure I was okay. He's always been like that—fiercely protective. Fearless. Never the type to back down, no matter who stood in front of him. But before anyone else made it to my bedside, he entered the room.

CHAPTER II: THE DREAMS CAME NEXT

A dark figure—silent, looming, familiar.

He stood at the foot of my bed, eyes heavy, mouth slightly open like he wanted to say something but just couldn't get the words out. The weight of guilt was draped over him like a shadow. I couldn't speak either. I just stared at him, trying to figure out what he wanted.

Then my son noticed him.

He didn't recognize the man, and like always, he got defensive. Protective. He squared up with him immediately, no hesitation, no fear.

I can't remember how the next part happened exactly, but something shifted—something dark and cruel.

The man issued a threat.

He told my son that if he didn't walk into the center of the hallway, if he didn't expose himself—he'd kill me.

And my son, without hesitation, obeyed. Not out of fear. Out of love.

He walked out into the hallway.

And the man shot him. Right there. No warning. No mercy.

He fell in the middle of that cold corridor.

No one could move. Not Pastor Danny. Not Josh. Not even me. They all stood there, paralyzed—impotent. No one could stop it.

And then I realized who the man was.

It was the same assassin from the Bronx—the one who had shot me and left me for dead. The one who started all of this, but this time, he hadn't come to kill me. He came to apologize.

He told me I wasn't the one who had ratted him out. That he had made a mistake. That everything that happened to me—the hit, the chaos, the paranoia—it was all wrong.

He wanted to make peace.

But instead... he took my son.

And I was left shattered. Broken in a way that no words could explain. Devastated in my soul.

In reality, I've never lost a child. Thank God. All three of my children are healthy, whole, and very much alive. But in that dream... the loss was real. The devastation felt total. The heartbreak lodged itself so deep in my subconscious that even after waking up—it didn't let go.

In this next dream, I had died.

It wasn't violent. It wasn't loud. It was quiet—peaceful even. There was no more pain. Just stillness.

I found myself standing somewhere... else. Somewhere light. And they were there—my family who had passed on. They were calling me home. Smiling. Reaching for me. Telling me it was okay. That it was time.

They were in heaven, or something like it. A place filled with warmth and acceptance. And I started walking toward them, crossing over from what I somehow knew was Earth 1... toward a second Earth. A better one. A final one.

But as I moved closer, I felt the pull—not from them, but from the other side. From Earth 1.

I couldn't do it.

I couldn't leave yet.

My kids were still there.

My daughters hadn't gotten married yet. I hadn't walked them down the aisle. I hadn't cried tears of joy seeing them in their white dresses, proud and broken in the best way a father is supposed to be in that moment. I hadn't held their hands before placing them into another's.

My grandchildren hadn't been born. I hadn't rocked them to sleep, or whispered secrets into their tiny ears about how

CHAPTER II: THE DREAMS CAME NEXT

strong and beautiful their parents were.

I hadn't grown old with my wife.

I hadn't held the door for her one more time as we got into the car. I hadn't kissed her forehead that morning after making coffee. I hadn't told her "I love you" one last time in the kind of way that settles into your bones and lingers for days.

And I wasn't ready to let go of that.

So I fought.

I pulled against the light, against the peace, against the warm voices telling me to come. I refused. I planted my spirit into the dirt of Earth 1 and refused to let go.

I wasn't done loving them yet.

Reflection

Some people say I died and came back.

Others tell me I was in limbo—caught somewhere between this world and the next.

I don't know which camp is right. Maybe both are wrong. Or maybe both are right in their own way.

What I do know—without a shadow of a doubt—is that I wasn't ready to leave my children.

Not yet.

I still had work to do. I still had lessons to teach, games to play, stories to tell. I still needed to hold them when they were hurting and celebrate them when they were flying. I still needed to show my son what a man should be, and remind my daughters what love is supposed to feel like.

I wanted to protect them.

I wanted to provide for them.

I wanted to love them—completely, fiercely, and without apology—until I knew they were good to stand on their own.

But there was something else, too.

I wasn't happy with the image I had left behind.

At that point in our lives, we were still living in poverty—struggling to make ends meet. I was working multiple jobs just to keep the lights on, to put food on the table. Driving deliveries late into the night. Working early mornings. Chasing every opportunity I could find, just to survive.

And I was tired.

Not just physically—spiritually.

But more than anything, I didn't want that to be the last memory my children had of me:

A man who was always working… but never had anything to show for it.

A man who gave everything but seemed stuck in place.

A man who meant well—but hadn't finished his story.

I wanted my son to see a man who was strong, who had purpose, and who saw things through to the end.

I wanted my daughters to look back and say, "Papi never gave up. He loved us with everything he had. He stayed."

I still had more to say.

More to give.

More to do.

So I stayed.

Chapter III: The Bedlam on Eldert

I don't remember every detail, but I remember the feeling. The streets of Bushwick were alive that night, but not in the usual way. Not the usual summertime energy, not the block party vibe with music bouncing off the brick buildings and cousins posted up on the stoop. This was something else—darker. Chaotic. Like war had broken out on Eldert Street.

We were scattered, moving in small packs like wolves, eyes sharp, hearts beating loud. I couldn't tell you exactly what triggered it, but I knew the reason: one of our own had been violated. One of our female cousins—one of our sisters, because that's what we are to each other—was accosted. And in our family, that doesn't go unanswered.

See, my grandfather on my mother's side had 36 kids. Thirty. Six. That means cousins by the dozens—an entire nation of us. It wasn't just one side. My paternal grandfather, Carlos Sánchez, had thirteen children with my grandmother. Both sides of my blood run deep. I come from two rivers, both wild and wide, and together they made an ocean of kin. A tribe. A fortress.

And that strength didn't start in Brooklyn. It started on the farmlands of the Dominican Republic.

My grandfather Carlos—my dad's father—was a farmer in

Gualete, up in the north near Puerto Plata. My mother's father was originally from Inoa and later settled in Yerba Buena. Both of them worked the land with their bare hands. They raised crops, they raised children, they raised legacies. They planted seeds that would grow into generations of warriors, lovers, thinkers, protectors. Men and women who knew how to fight, how to pray, how to love, and how to survive.

Eldert Street? That was more than just a block in Brooklyn. That was our turf. That's where my grandfather Carlos lived. It's where I spent some of the best days of my childhood—birthday parties, domino games, cookouts, cousins packed into rooms like sardines, laughter bouncing off the walls. It was sacred ground. And that made what happened in the dream feel even more personal. Even more painful.

We weren't out for blood that night. We were just out for justice. We wanted answers. Respect. But those other kats didn't move with the same code. They brought a gun to a fist fight.

One shot. That's all it took. My cousin Shorty went down, and the whole scene turned surreal. Screams. Footsteps. Somebody calling for an ambulance. My ears were ringing, my body frozen. I remember grabbing him, trying to keep pressure on the wound, trying to talk to him, to keep him here.

And then—it was like my eyes became a drone camera. The chaos stayed on the ground, but I was lifting, drifting. Floating upward, slowly rising away from the flashing lights and sirens. Away from the pain and the noise. The streetlights turned to stars. The shouts faded to silence.

I was leaving Eldert... but I wasn't waking up. I was just moving on to the next layer of this dreamscape. The next world. The next trial.

Chapter IV: The Backyard Beyond

After the chaos on Eldert, after the gunshot and the slow drift into the night sky, I didn't wake up.
I died again.
Or at least, it felt like it.
This wasn't the first time I dreamed I had died and was on my way to heaven. In a previous dream, I remember being welcomed by family—warm, familiar faces inviting me to come home, to stay. But even then, I couldn't do it. I couldn't leave my wife. I couldn't leave my children.
This time, though, I didn't get a chance to say no. I didn't argue or beg. I was just there—in my grandfather's backyard on Eldert Street. The place that, for me, was heaven on earth.
Everything looked like I was seeing it through a warm, cloudy filter. Like I was inside a memory but still somehow alive in it. The details were hazy, but the presence of everyone was crystal clear. I knew who they were. I could feel the love, the history, the safety of it all.
We were all there—my whole family. Primos, tías, tíos. It was a classic summer scene: dominoes clacking, someone laughing too loud, smoke from the grill drifting through the yard, old heads telling stories half in Spanish, half in Spanglish, all of it magic. "¿Te recuerda' de esa ve' que..." and "¡Muchacho, tú

no sabe' nada!" followed by someone busting out laughing or shaking their head with a smirk.

In our family, Spanish is the language of expression. It's how we were raised, how we love, how we roast each other, how we pray. When the older generation talks, it's all español—rich, fast, full of dichos that only make sense if you've lived both struggle and joy in the same sentence. With the cousins, it's a mix—bouncing between English and Spanish like we were born with a switch we can flip mid-thought. We straddle the line between both worlds, between "yo bro" and "oye loco," between "that's wild" and "¡Diablo, qué vaina!"

To outsiders it probably sounds like a mess. To us, it's poetry. A river with two currents, both flowing in the same direction.

I didn't want to leave.

That backyard holds a kind of peace I can't explain. It's the soil where so much of our love was planted. Summers with all the cousins, packed into the basement like there was no place else to be, playing Nintendo for hours. Watching my uncle Ivan absolutely dominate every classic game you could think of— Megaman, Zelda, Metroid, Ikari Warriors, Ninja Gaiden. He was the GOAT. We called him "The Master" because he didn't just play—he conquered. His victories were our victories. We'd sit around him in awe, cheering like he just won the World Series.

Of course, we'd fight over who had next. And being the youngest in the crew? Yeah, I got played. I used to hate it, being at the bottom of the food chain. But over time, I stopped caring about the controller. I just wanted to be there. With them. In that space. In that love.

We bonded over everything—video games, baseball, football, games of gesture, bubble gum, fart wars (yeah, I said it), cartoons,

CHAPTER IV: THE BACKYARD BEYOND

and music. It was ours.

Love took root there. In the long summer days and cold winter nights. In the football games we played on the block and in the living room—until we broke grandma's couch.

Yo... we were terrified. We thought we were dead for real.

We... (not me but somebody hehehe) caught a whoopin', no doubt. But we survived. And somehow, that made the memory even sweeter. That was childhood. That was family.

And in that dream, standing in my grandfather's backyard, surrounded by all of them... I felt it again. That pure, unfiltered gratitude. That deep knowing that I was loved. That I came from something strong. That heaven might just look a whole lot like a backyard in Bushwick.

Chapter V: The Smell of Death

After lingering in the love of my family, bathed in the warm haze of childhood summers and Spanglish laughter in my grandfather's backyard, I was lifted again. Transported. This time, to a place that felt completely foreign.

I was in what I understood to be Sri Lanka, deep in the desert, in a massive complex—like some futuristic monastery meets Google headquarters. And in this reality, I wasn't just a part of something. I was the thing. A big-time CEO. A man who had built an empire. Accomplished. Powerful. Respected.

But also... severely obese.

So large, in fact, that I had to be carted around in an electronic chair. I had a robot assistant that looked like something straight out of I, Robot—white chrome frame, glowing blue core, and an eerie monotone voice that followed me wherever I went. It managed my schedule, executed my wishes, and— unfortunately—was programmed to handle my death.

That day, I was giving a presentation in the boardroom about the etymology of my wife's name—Alejandra. It was elegant. Intentional. A labor of love. I had constructed the most beautiful presentation, rich with historical meaning. I traced the name back to its Greek roots—Alexandros, "defender of man"—and I spoke with reverence about how that meaning

CHAPTER V: THE SMELL OF DEATH

manifested in her posture, her strength, her fierce and quiet protection of me in real life. She had always guarded me—seen things I couldn't, shielded me in ways I never fully understood until much later. This was my tribute to her.

And then... I died.

Right there mid-presentation. Just paused. Froze. Everything still. The people in the room stared at me, unsure if it was part of the show. And then my robot turned toward them and said, flatly:

"The proprietor has expired."

No panic. No drama. Just procedure.

The board members sighed like a meeting had been canceled. They were escorted out, and the robot initiated a carefully designed protocol. My final wishes. The first task: get my body to the roll-out room.

That's where things got... weird.

I was taken to this sterile chamber—cold, metallic, humming with a low frequency—and handed over to a man who I didn't know. For the sake of my sanity, I called him Phil. Phil's job was to roll me around this strange, draining chamber so that the liquid I was full of—my life force, my essence, my bile—could be completely extracted. The last step before I could transition to whatever came next.

So there I was, limp, massive, and leaking into the floor while Phil methodically sloshed me around like I was a damn bowling ball. Every turn spilled more of that bile into the drain. With each ounce lost, I felt myself slipping.

But then came the shift.

Suddenly, I wasn't in the roll-out room anymore. I was someone else. A white guy in the Midwest, speeding down a highway in a T-top with a gorgeous blonde cheerleader in the passenger seat. Windows down. Hair blowing in the wind. Classic rock blasting through the speakers. We were living.

And then—her nose wrinkled.

She turned to me with that look, you know the one, and said: "What is that smell?"

I was confused. I sniffed myself. Took a look around. Didn't seem like anything was off... or at least, that's what that version of me could tell.

Then—snap—I was back in the roll-out room, watching from a third-person perspective. Watching myself being drained by Phil. Watching the floor slick with the fluid of my fading life. And it hit me.

The smell she noticed? It was death.

My decay. From this side of the dream. The two realities were bleeding into each other.

It happened again. I jumped back to the Midwest, now in a bedroom with the same blonde girl. We were being intimate, but she paused again—same look of disgust.

"What is that smell?"

She didn't understand it, but I was starting to. Something was rotting in the other world, and it was starting to show. I was rotting.

Then, one last shift.

This time I was back in the Midwest again, but now we were in what looked like a high school chemistry lab. She was there. So was her friend. I was still holding onto that version of reality by a thread, but the dream was coming undone.

Back in the roll-out room, Phil was almost finished. Just a few more ounces left to drain. And as he emptied the last bit of bile, my Midwestern self collapsed, seizing violently. The blonde and her friend backed away in horror.

CHAPTER V: THE SMELL OF DEATH

And then it happened—a rupture.

Like a wormhole had opened, and for the first time, the two realities weren't just overlapping—they were connected. She saw through. She smelled through. And she realized the truth: her boyfriend was tied to a decaying corpse in another world.

Me.

It was surreal—living across realities, bleeding through timelines, collapsing into myself as my spirit and flesh were slowly being emptied. I thought it was all symbolic. Some elaborate metaphor cooked up by my subconscious to represent letting go.

But when I told my wife about the dream later, she just nodded. Quiet. Thoughtful.

Then she said, "They rolled you like that because you were in a prone position."

I blinked. "What?"

She explained that during the early days of Covid, patients who were intubated and in critical condition were often placed on their stomachs—proned—to help their lungs expand and get oxygen flowing. Nurses and techs would rotate you every few hours. Sometimes side to side. Sometimes face-down. Always careful. Always hoping it would help.

And it clicked.

The "roll out room." The draining. Phil, my unknown caretaker, sloshing me around like I was a giant container of bile. It wasn't just a dream. It was a translation of something real—something happening to me in that hospital room. My body was being moved in hopes of saving me, while my spirit was caught somewhere between realities.

But the weight of that realization didn't stop there.

My wife had already seen the virus take someone she loved.

Her father was admitted to a hospital in the Bronx—a different borough, a different building, but the same war. He had slipped into a coma one week before I did. While I lay unconscious in one hospital surrounded by machines and silence, he lay in his own hospital bed in the Bronx, fighting the same invisible enemy.

And for him... there was no waking up. No second chance. He passed away two weeks into my coma.

My wife didn't tell me right away. She waited. She held that grief quietly, locked it inside while I healed. She didn't want to overwhelm me. Didn't want to burden my recovery with more sorrow. She chose to carry that weight alone for a while—just like she always did. Protecting me. Shielding me. Standing in the gap, as she had so many times before.

More on that later.

In that dream—when the smell of death crossed dimensions and the veil between life and decay began to lift—I believe some part of me felt that something had been lost. That someone sacred had passed on.

Chapter VI: What Covid Took

Finding out that my father-in-law died while I was in the coma—and that I wasn't there to support my wife through it—broke me.

Since the day we got married, I had already told myself: When the day comes, I'll be there. I would be the rock she leaned on when she lost her parents. I would hold her. Pray with her. Speak life when grief comes to the door. That was the role I had taken on willingly, gladly, lovingly.

But Covid stole that from me.

While I lay unconscious in a hospital bed in Manhattan—first at NY Presbyterian in Queens, then transferred to Cornell, and finally to the Hospital for Special Surgery—her father lay dying in the Bronx. Two boroughs apart. Two comas. Two completely different outcomes.

She had to absorb the loss of her father alone. Not just the man who gave her life, but the man who had become her friend again. Her comfort. Her daddy. She had to cry without me. She had to make arrangements and decisions without my arms around her. She had to keep breathing while holding space for the unthinkable possibility that the father of her children might die too. She had to carry all of that. And still hope.

And if that wasn't enough—she was denied even the chance

to say goodbye.

There was no wake. No funeral. No option to view the body. The hospital protocols were strict. The body was cremated, fast, with no ceremony, no invitation, no final moment of dignity. His wife—her stepmother—made the arrangements and didn't provide the opportunity for his children to mourn him properly. The whole thing was stripped of humanity. The ritual of grief was cut short, like an unfinished prayer.

So my wife didn't just lose her father—she lost the process of grieving him. She was left holding a silence too big to name, with no space to release it.

And I wasn't there.

That's the part that still haunts me. That I couldn't stand beside her. That I couldn't wipe her tears or speak life over her when she needed it most. She had to carry her own heartbreak and the fear of losing me too.

And I loved her father. I truly did.

He was my dad joke partner. Our humor was the same—corny, goofy, perfect. My wife always said she married her father because I told the same dumb jokes. We'd laugh at things nobody else did. He and I shared that lightness.

He had his demons, no doubt. He wasn't always the best father or husband. But toward the end, he tried. And as a follower of Jesus, I believe in that. In redemption. In mercy. In grace. God teaches us to love instead of hate, to build instead of break down. And in those last five years, he honored his role. He became the father my wife needed. A true confidant. A protector. A man doing the work. Her daddy.

And for that—I am deeply grateful.

Every daughter deserves to hold a good image of her father in her heart. Not a perfect one, but a redeemed one. And I

CHAPTER VI: WHAT COVID TOOK

thank God that my wife got to have that. At least five really good years.

Still, what Covid took can't be overstated.
It didn't just take lives.
It robbed us of the rituals of healing.
It robbed us of the holding.
The hugging.
The goodbyes.
And those losses… they echo.

Chapter VII: The Doorway of Paradise... Forgiveness

My body was done.

In the dream, my corpse was being carted out of the roll-out room—limp, formless, a pile of loose flesh wrapped in a white sheet. Phil handed me off to another man—big guy, big hands—and this dude rolled me through a nameless corridor flooded with bright lights. I looked like I had already crossed over. But there was one more task to be done.

Without warning, he began to push his finger into my rectum.

The discomfort was indescribable. It wasn't just physical—it was violating. I was disgusted. Outraged. After everything I'd already been through—the loss, the pain, the chaos, the dying—I now had to suffer this indignity?

Apparently, I still had some bile left. And his job—however cruel it felt—was to finish the process. Drain the last bit. Because I wasn't completely dead yet. I was stuck between this world and the next.

And then, in an instant, I was no longer in that corridor.

I was standing in the most pristine, luminous space I had ever seen. A massive, radiant room, filled with pure light—no shadows, no edges. It felt... perfect. Sacred. Peaceful. At the far end was a single doorway, and in front of it stood a massive

CHAPTER VII: THE DOORWAY OF PARADISE... FORGIVENESS

silver cross. It reflected light so intensely I could barely keep my eyes on it. But I was drawn to it. Drawn like a child drawn home.

As I moved closer, I heard a voice. The Voice.

God.

It wasn't frightening—it was familiar. I knew it. And that knowing gave me peace. The Bible says, "My sheep know my voice"—and in that moment, I knew I was one of His. I had been walking the right path. Stumbling, yes. Imperfect, always. But in relationship with Him. And He was here.

He asked me:

"Are you ready to enter into your rest?"

I exhaled.

"Yes... I am."

As I answered, I watched the silver cross begin to turn crimson—like it was being baptized in the blood of Jesus. The red moved slowly, like a holy wave washing over the metal. But just before it reached the center, it stopped.

Then God said:

"Before you can enter, you have to forgive the person who killed your son."

I froze.

My spirit clenched. My face twisted. I was dumbfounded. That wasn't what I expected. It hit me like a blow to the chest. Not because I hadn't heard God ask hard things before—but because this was different. Deep. Painful. Personal.

I stood there in stunned silence. Then, with frustration bubbling up, I finally said:

"(sigh)... Yo God... you gotta give me a minute, bro. That's... that's big. Give me a second, please?"

And just like He always does—He waited. Patient. Gentle.

Understanding. He gave me time. Maybe in heaven it was just a few seconds. On Earth? Maybe 200 years. I don't know. But eventually, the Spirit within me surrendered.

"Ok... I forgive him."

And the moment I said those words, the cross became completely covered in red. The blood of Christ now enveloping the symbol of my salvation. And I heard the voice say:

"You may enter into your rest."

That was the moment I woke up.

April 9, 2020. ICU. Manhattan. No more dreams. No more metaphors. Just cold air, blinking monitors, cables everywhere, a plastic apparatus in my mouth, a feeding tube, an arterial line in my neck and left hand. Wrappings around my legs to prevent clots.

I had returned.

But I hadn't crossed into paradise. Not yet. I had re-entered the battlefield of recovery. And I would soon discover that the journey ahead would be just as hard—if not harder—than the one I had just survived in my own mind.

Chapter VIII: Back to "reality"?

That grief followed me back into the real world.
When I finally came out of the coma, disoriented, weak, unsure of what was real and what was imagined, the pain of losing my son was still with me. It clung to my chest like it had happened yesterday—because in my mind, it had. I didn't know the difference.
Then came the first FaceTime call.
My wife and kids were on the other end of the screen. Faces I hadn't seen in what felt like a lifetime. And there—right in the middle—was my son.
Alive. Breathing. Real.
I was shocked. Overwhelmed. My voice cracked as I asked, almost in disbelief:
"Son... you're alive!???"
They all looked at me like I had lost my mind. Maybe, in that moment, I had. Just a little. The line between the dream world and reality had blurred, and I didn't know what was true anymore.
But what I did know—what I felt—was relief. Pure, soul-deep gratitude. The kind of thankfulness that only comes after believing you've lost everything and being given a second chance.

That moment stays with me.

I'll never forget it for as long as I live.

I opened my eyes on April 9th, 2020—but I hadn't fully come back. Not really. My body was awake. The machines had done their part. But my mind, my spirit… they were still floating somewhere between dreams, drenched in parables and pain and holy encounters I couldn't explain. The world I returned to felt unreal, like waking up on the wrong set of a movie I didn't remember auditioning for. I was alive—but I was still in limbo.

I had left the coma… but the coma hadn't completely left me.

Chapter IX: Back from the Edge: Leg Raises and Hallucinations

April 9th, 2020. I didn't know what day it was when I opened my eyes—I didn't even know how much time had passed. All I knew was that the dreams I had just experienced weren't just dreams. They were real. I had lived them. I had been shot 22 times in a hospital room in Detroit. A badass Mexican nurse had saved me from blue-haired nurses trying to suffocate me. My son had died. And somehow, I was still in Sri Lanka.

I woke up certain of all of it. It wasn't until I began to scan my surroundings that the truth started to press in. I was in a hospital room—an ICU. There were four or five other patients around me, all critically ill. The room was rectangular, and I was positioned along the left wall, just a few feet from the door that led to the hallway. In the center of the space was a small nurse station with a large window—probably a two-way mirror—where people could monitor vitals and room activity.

Now here's the thing—I believed there were three guys behind that mirror. In my mind, they were avid fans of hip hop and hood culture, watching me, judging me, trying to validate whether or not I truly had a "hood card." It was weird, but it made sense in the world my mind was still in. I would have these imagined interactions with them, casual at first, but they would eventually evolve into something way more intense during one of the hallucinations that came later. But at that moment, they were just three IT dudes in a secret little office overlooking the ICU, watching from their booth.

All the medical staff appeared to be of Indian descent. One man wore a turban, and his skin had an orange hue—probably from an antiseptic coating used to prevent infection. But in my mind, it had something to do with... I don't even know what. My mind was still convinced I was in Sri Lanka. My last dream had me as a CEO of a major company there, and the illusion hadn't yet broken.

Now here's the thing—after being intubated, your voice changes. It gets raspy, dry, almost whispery. Think Batman in The Dark Knight. Cool if you're doing a movie monologue. Terrible if you're trying to make sense.

So there I was, barely able to speak, yet determined. I called a nurse over and rasped out the most urgent thing I could think of: "I need to use your phone. I have to call the embassy to get back to the States."

He nodded quickly. "Yes, of course. Just give us some time. You have to rest." Then he walked away.

In my head, I was yelling: WTF!? Why was this guy ignoring me? I'd been gone from my family for what felt like forever.

I asked another nurse—same response. This one at least rubbed my shoulder, which gave me a sliver of comfort. Then came this super muscular nurse—also Indian, mad chill. When I spoke to him, he actually listened, nodded like he believed me. That small act of kindness gave me peace. I really thought he was going to help me get in touch with the embassy.

At some point, they removed the plastic bracket still in my mouth—the thing that had held the respiratory tube in place.

CHAPTER IX: BACK FROM THE EDGE: LEG RAISES AND...

It was uncomfortable as hell. But once it was gone, my mind shifted: I had to get strong. I had to recover. I had to get out of this bed and back to the good ol' United States of America.

Now, unless you've been in a coma—or know someone who has—let me break it down for you: when you're inactive that long, your muscles shut down. It's called muscle atrophy, and it's no joke. You don't just lose your strength—you lose your ability to do anything that requires muscle control. I'm not talking squats or bench presses. I'm talking about basic things: standing up, wiping your own ass, brushing your teeth, holding a spoon, sending a text.

I couldn't feed myself. My hands trembled violently just trying to grip a utensil. The tiny muscles that control small movements were wrecked. That experience made me appreciate things I never gave a second thought to. The simple stuff. Wiping after using the bathroom. Holding my phone. Writing a message. Eating.

But I wasn't about to let that stop me. I was determined to rebuild. I started doing leg raises in bed. Mini pull-ups using the rings above me. Anything to activate those dormant muscles.

The nurses told me I needed to take it easy. They begged me to stop.

But I whispered, with all the fire I could muster: "Hell no. This is what I need to do to get the hell out of this bed. I'm going home to my family, and this is how I do it."

Now, in my heart, I screamed that line. In reality, it came out like a hoarse whisper. But it didn't matter. I meant every word. That was just the first few hours after waking up... then came the hallucinations.

Chapter X: Post-ICU Hallucinations

That first day was weird—really weird. I was awake, aware, and fully convinced I was somewhere overseas. I kept trying to get the hospital personnel to bring me a phone so I could call the U.S. embassy. I was dead serious. Every time I asked, they gave me that soft, polite nod—"Yes, absolutely. We'll get the embassy on the line as soon as they're available." But of course, they never did.

Then the hallucinations started.

At first, they were beautiful. Comforting, even. I saw my entire family in the room with me—my mom, my aunts, my uncles, cousins. All of them. It felt like a big Dominican reunion right there in the ICU. They were laughing, chatting, planning a party to celebrate my recovery. It was like I'd already made it out of the woods. And the best part? They said Juan Luis Guerra was coming to perform.

Man, I was hyped. That's one of my favorite artists of all time. Just the idea of hearing "Bachata Rosa" or "Ojalá Que Llueva Café" live had me smiling from ear to ear—even if I could barely move.

But then... the dream twisted.

Somehow, I had beef with the Triad. Yeah. The Triad gangs were trying to kill me. Don't ask how we got from Juan Luis

CHAPTER X: POST-ICU HALLUCINATIONS

Guerra to international organized crime—this was coma logic, where one second you're dancing, and the next you're dodging bullets.

There was this Asian dude standing outside my ICU door. One of the guys from that little room behind the two-way mirror. I recognized him somehow—he'd been part of the hospital staff, maybe security. But in the hallucination, he was there with a .22 caliber pistol, trying to shoot me because I had "snitched" on him for stealing my laptop. He'd gotten fired over it, and now he wanted revenge. Eff that guy he stole my laptop and I wanted it back.

He started banging on the ICU door, pistol in hand. I was defenseless. I couldn't even sit up on my own, much less fight. But outta nowhere, my cousin—ride or die—steps in and starts fighting him. I could hear them. The struggle. The grunts. The fists hitting flesh. My cousin's voice rang out as clear as my own breath.

And then... the gunshot.

I swear to you, I heard the shot. Heard my cousin's body hit the ground outside my door. That sound will never leave me. Something inside me snapped. I was frantic. I had to help. I tried to get out of the bed, legs shaking, lungs working overtime. My heart was racing and the machines I was connected to were going crazy, but I didn't care. My cousin was dying, and I wasn't about to just lie there.

The doctor was yelling at me to calm down. "Your blood pressure is too high! Heart rate's at 110!" they warned. But I couldn't stop. I threw one leg over the bed, tried to plant it on the ground. Nothing. I had no strength. But I kept fighting. I had to.

Then, thank God, my other cousin arrived. He jumped in,

fought the guy, and took him down. Moments later, my cop friend Rocky showed up—badge out, cool as ever—and arrested the dude on the spot. I was safe.

Rocky stayed with me. He didn't leave. Once the situation "cleared," he personally wheeled me out of the ICU to the new COVID ward. I was officially in the post-ICU hallway, a makeshift ward packed with recovering patients. It wasn't glamorous, but to me, it felt like the first step toward going home.

As Rocky pushed my bed through the hallway, I spotted two nurses nearby. Both women. Both with blue hair—just like the ones from Detroit. My heart skipped. I told Rocky about them, about how I'd seen them before and didn't trust them.

He put a hand on my shoulder and said, "Don't worry, bro. I got you. You're safe now."

And for the first time that day, I believed it.

Everything in me — my nerves, my doubt, my racing thoughts — took a breath.

Not because the nurses disappeared. Not because I understood what was real.

But because he said I was safe. And I trusted him.

Rocky, if you ever read this... Thank you. Even though you were a hallucination in that moment, you gave me peace when it was hard to find it. I've always appreciated your friendship and I hope you and Jo are well brother, God bless you mightily.

Hallway Recovery...

After they moved me out of the ICU, I wasn't taken straight to a room.

I was wheeled into a hallway, where I remained for three or four days.

But let me say this clearly:

CHAPTER X: POST-ICU HALLUCINATIONS

I was never alone.
The hospital staff — those angels in scrubs — took extraordinary care of me.
They waved. They smiled. They encouraged me daily.
Even though they were running on fumes, working through the worst crisis of their lives,
they poured themselves into me with compassion, patience, and faith.
"You're strong," they'd say. "You got this."
Not once did I feel forgotten. Not once did they treat me like an afterthought.
They were tired — I could see it in their eyes —
but they never stopped shining.
You can't do that job without love.
Real love. God's love.
And they had it in abundance.
Eventually, they moved me into a shared room.
My roommate was a gentle, thoughtful man recovering from COVID —
not physically wrecked the way I had been,
but still sick, still fighting his own battle.
And in the middle of his recovery,
he was planning his father's funeral.
I listened as he made arrangements from his hospital bed.
Soft-voiced, composed, and somehow still encouraging me.
Even in his grief, he checked in on me.
Spoke kindness into my confusion.
Offered hope without even knowing how much I needed it.
I couldn't hold anything in my hands without trembling violently.
My body still didn't belong to me.

But I had enough strength to reach for my phone...
and listen.
Voicemail after voicemail.
My wife. My children. My parents. Aunts. Uncles. Friends. Coworkers.
Pedro Almonte, the owner of the bodega at the corner.
Billy. G. James. Kin. Yari. The guys from John Adams.
Prayers. Cries. Encouragement.
Some voices were steady. Some cracked with emotion.
But all of them were planted with love.
I had the whole world praying for me.
And I heard it — in every word, every pause, every tear they tried to hide.
I still have those voicemails.
I'll never delete them.
They're living proof that every moment we share with another human being matters.
That every act of love, every hello, every seed of kindness — it all comes back when it matters most.
The seeds we plant in the hearts of others today...
become the prayers we reap tomorrow.

Chapter XI: The Room with a View...

They eventually moved me into a room. And not just any room — this one had a view of the East River that could quiet a storm.

Sunrises and sunsets painted across the sky like God was showing off.

But as beautiful as it was, it also shook me.

I've been a New Yorker my whole life.

I know what the FDR looks like on a regular day — bumper to bumper, taxis weaving, ambulances screaming by.

But during the pandemic?

It was empty.

A ghost road in a ghost city.

It felt like I was watching a post-apocalyptic movie — only I was in it.

Alive. But not fully back.

Despite the eeriness, there were bright spots.

Like the food.

I know what you're thinking — hospital food is supposed to be nasty.

But let me tell you something about the Hospital for Special Surgery...

Their food was BANGIN.

Like, I'd-eat-this-if-I-wasn't-dying bangin.

But because I had been intubated, they kept me on a liquid diet to avoid choking.

That was torture.

I was jonesin' for solid food.

And when I finally got the green light, I don't even remember what they gave me — I just remember it tasted like freedom.

That moment became one of my short-term goals — I made a list.

Small wins I could control.

Benchmarks on the way back to me.

Solid food ✓

Wipe my own ass

Walk on my own

Shower… dear God, let me shower

If you know me, you know I don't go a day without a shower.

At that point, I hadn't bathed in almost a month.

I didn't stink — they were flushing toxins from my system via feeding tubes — but I felt filthy.

Showering is more than hygiene for me.

It's sacred.

It's symbolic.

It's the moment where I wash off the world — the dust, the stress, the sin, the sorrow.

And I missed it like oxygen.

So I asked the nurses.

"Can I please take a shower?"

They looked at me with sympathy and love, but the answer was always the same:

"You're a fall risk. The doctor has to approve it."

So I went to the doctor.

Pled my case like a lawyer.

CHAPTER XI: THE ROOM WITH A VIEW...

"Put a plastic chair in the shower," I said. "I'll sit. Let a nurse stay nearby. I just need to feel water on my skin."
He paused.
"I'll discuss it with the team," he said.
My heart jumped.
Around the same time, they brought a walker into my room.
Game on.
I started training.
Doing dips.
Taking steps.
Pacing the floor, refusing to rest.
I would not stay in that bed.
I would not go one more day without a shower.
Eventually, I worked up the strength to walk to the sink, brush my teeth, and walk back.
It wrecked me, but I did it.
I asked again.
And finally — permission granted.
The nurse came in with a full setup:
A basin.
Body wash.
Shampoo.
Conditioner.
Lotion.
Clean socks.
Toothpaste.
You would've thought I'd won the lottery.
When I finally sat in that chair and felt the first drops of water hit my head...
I kid you not — it was better than sex.
The water ran down my scalp, over my shoulders, down to

my toes.

And with it went fear, anger, frustration, pain, and disappointment.

That wasn't just a shower.

It was a baptism.

I wasn't healed yet.

But I was cleansed.

And I was on my way.

Night sweats...

Eventually, the man sharing the room with me was discharged.

And for the first time since waking from my coma...

I was alone.

No more monitors beeping from the next bed.

No more quiet encouragement from someone fighting his own battle.

Just me.

And the silence.

Funny thing about silence —

it's never truly quiet.

During the day, there were distractions.

Nurses. Doctors. Physical therapy.

The rhythm of recovery kept me tethered to reality.

But at night...

that silence turned into an amplifier.

It turned up the volume on my thoughts, my regrets, my fears.

All of it came flooding in.

I was still reconciling what was real and what wasn't.

I had moments of clarity during the day —

little anchors offered by the people around me,

but when the sun dipped below the horizon...

CHAPTER XI: THE ROOM WITH A VIEW...

I was floating again.
Every two hours like clockwork, I'd wake up in a panic.
Soaked in sweat. Shivering. Terrified.
Trying to convince myself this wasn't another hallucination.
Trying to believe I was awake. That I had survived.
But my body didn't believe it yet.
And sometimes... neither did I.
One night, around 4 a.m., I woke up drenched again —
gown and sheets soaked through, hands shaking, heart racing.
And without even thinking, I reached for my phone.
I called the only person I knew could ground me:
my mother.
Normally she would've scolded me for waking her up that early.
But that night?
I got a different version of her —
a mother who had stared down the very real possibility of losing her son,
and now knew what mattered most.
Her voice was soft.
Steady.
Sacred.
I don't remember everything I said,
but I know I opened with what I always say when I call:
"Ción, mami..."
And then, with a trembling voice:
"Am I awake? Is this real?"
I can't quote her exact reply.
But I remember the feeling.
Peace.
That night, she gave me exactly what I needed.

And when we hung up, I called the nurse.
Asked her to please bring me a fresh gown and change the sheets.
Because I couldn't lay there in fear-soaked linen for another second.
That was the night I realized recovery wasn't just about walking again...
It was about believing I was still here.
But some nights...
even after the phone call, even after the clean sheets,
the fear would creep back in.
And I did the only thing I could:
I prayed.
I wasn't praying like some spiritual giant.
I was praying like a man dangling by a thread —
still caught between coma dreams and the real world,
still unsure if I had truly made it out.
In the dark, I whispered:
"God, I believe You are powerful. I believe You can do great things...
but please... help my unbelief."
Just like that man in the Gospel who stood before Jesus —
desperate, doubting, and honest.
That was me.
A broken disciple in a hospital bed,
begging not for healing this time...
but for faith to believe I'd already been healed.
And you know what?
He heard me.
Not in a thunderclap. Not with angels descending.
But in the stillness.

CHAPTER XI: THE ROOM WITH A VIEW...

In the fact that I made it through that night.
And the next one.
And the one after that.

Chapter XII: "Ginger" The Red Nurse...

By then, my recovery was becoming steady.
I was walking more. Eating more. My mind was clearer.
But not everything was smooth.
One concern kept lingering — my heart rate.
Even at rest, it clocked in at 110 beats per minute.
Too fast. Too risky.
A cardiologist came in to evaluate me.
He explained that the sac around my heart was filled with fluid,
a condition known as pericardial effusion —
not uncommon after a traumatic illness like the one I had just survived.
It wasn't life-threatening at that point, but it was enough to delay my release.
I understood. But emotionally?
It crushed me.
I missed my family.
I missed my friends.
I missed warmth — the sound of laughter in the room,
the feeling of hugs and daps,
the invisible joy that comes from being surrounded by people

CHAPTER XII: "GINGER" THE RED NURSE...

you love.
But now?
Physical touch was off-limits.
The pandemic had turned us all into strangers in our own skin.
Hugs became hazards.
Proximity became dangerous.
I'm a tactile person.
I grew up in a culture where we kiss cheeks, dap hands, slap backs,
hold each other when words fail.
So this sterile, gloved, double-masked world?
It felt like prison.
And then she walked in.
A nurse — white, red hair, kind eyes.
Gentle in tone, firm in knowledge, and full of something different. She moved confidently like a woman who's weathered some storms but came out on top. Her kindness was seasoned with the experience and service of motherhood and it came out of her in droves.
She told me that her entire family had already had COVID.
They were asymptomatic, and she had continued to work through it.
One day, she walked into my room —
no gloves. No mask.
I was floored.
The audacity. The humanity. The reckless, beautiful compassion.
I LOVED her.
She came to take my vitals,
and when she reached for my wrist with her bare hand,

I cried.
It was the first time in weeks I had felt another human being's touch —
not through latex, not through protocol,
but real, honest, skin-to-skin human contact.
She didn't rush.
She held my hand.
And she stood there while I wept.
I was afraid for her.
Afraid I might harm her.
So through the tears, I asked:
"Are you going to be okay?"
She smiled gently and said:
"I'm immune."
That moment did something to me.
It healed a part of me that medicine couldn't reach.
To that nurse — wherever you are... I pray God blesses you immensely.
You didn't just take my vitals.
You gave me life.
Thank you.
I've grown to understand that God doesn't just speak through scripture or sermons.
Sometimes, He sends a nurse with red hair and no gloves.
Sometimes, His love shows up as a bare hand on a trembling wrist.
That moment reminded me:
Presence is everything.
To be present — truly present — in every moment of everyday life is vital.
We spend so much time on our phones, behind screens,

CHAPTER XII: "GINGER" THE RED NURSE...

distracted and disengaged,
that we forfeit the very thing that fuels our growth and transformation.
The conflict.
The tension.
The misunderstandings, debates, and arguments —
they're not interruptions to the process.
They are the process.
We can't grow without friction.
We can't mature without struggle.
And we can't truly love without first choosing to show up — fully, vulnerably, and without armor.
That red-headed nurse didn't just take my vitals.
She was present.
And in that presence, I felt God.
Not in a sermon.
Not in a vision.
But in a bare hand, extended in compassion,
reminding me that even in the shadow of death,
I was still alive.
Even in isolation, I was never truly alone.

Chapter XIII: Requiem for the living

April 20th, 2020.
 Six days after my birthday.
 But it felt like I had been born again.
 After everything — the coma, the tubes, the walker, the trauma, the slow crawl back to life —
 I was finally going home.
 I was excited.
 So excited.
 To breathe real air.
 To feel sunlight on my skin without a hospital window in the way.
 To see my daughters. Eat a home cooked meal.
 To simply not be dying.
 But joy never comes alone.
 Alongside the hope was a quiet current of anxiety.
 My wife and I still hadn't reconciled.
 She had refused to engage in deep conversation while I was recovering,
 and while that frustrated me, I also knew it was kindness disguised as distance.
 She didn't want to burden me during my recovery.
 Even though our marriage was hanging by threads, she still

CHAPTER XIII: REQUIEM FOR THE LIVING

put my healing above her hurt.
I'll always be grateful for that.
Before I left, there was one final moment I didn't expect.
Lou Shapiro, president of the Hospital for Special Surgery, came to see me.
The president. Of the whole hospital.
He sat down — not to lecture, not to give a PR handshake — but to talk.
To ask about my life. My story. My family.
He was kind. Gentle. Curious. Human.
We stayed in touch for a while after that.
I'd send him emails from time to time — just saying thank you.
Eventually, he stepped down to enjoy retirement,
but I'll never forget how present he was in that moment.
Thank you, Lou.
For seeing me. For caring. For running a hospital filled with angels.
When it was finally time to leave, I was wheeled out through the main corridor.
Per hospital protocol, I had to go out in a chair —
but I wasn't alone.
There was a line of nurses, doctors, and staff waiting for me.
Clapping. Smiling. Crying.
Celebrating.
After all the death they had seen —
I was a win.
A rare victory in a war they were still losing daily.
I didn't go home in a car.
There was no one waiting outside with balloons.
Instead, two paramedics loaded me into an ambulance

and drove me back to Bushwick.
When we got to my building, they offered to carry me up the three flights of stairs.
But I looked at them and said:
"I'm a grown-ass man. You ain't carrying me up nothin'. I'm walking."
They laughed. "Alright bro… you got it."
And with my walker in hand,
one paramedic behind me, one in front,
I made that climb.
Step by burning step.
Every muscle on fire.
But I made it.
I had lost 40 pounds in the hospital.
I was back to 187 — the weight I hadn't seen since freshman year of college.
Rockstar skinny.
Empty tank.
But I was home.
And waiting at the top of the stairs?
My kids.
They had decorated the apartment.
Made a cake.
Wrote me a card.
They didn't care that I looked like a skeleton with a beard.
They didn't care that I was walking slow.
They were just happy I was back.
And that day —
We celebrated what we could.
There were decorations, cake, and laughter.
There were hugs I thought I might never feel again.

CHAPTER XIII: REQUIEM FOR THE LIVING

There was music, movement, and joy in the air —
but beneath all of it, a quiet ache lingered.
Because even in that moment of resurrection,
someone was still missing.
Just weeks earlier, my wife's father, Felix Escoto Sr., had passed from COVID-19.
A man whose story had been scarred by addiction and failure —
but also marked by redemption.
He had been an alcoholic, an absent father, a source of deep pain...
but in his later years, something shifted.
He started reaching out.
Started listening.
Started making things right — especially with his little girl.
And as a father myself, I understood that hunger.
That need to restore what we've broken.
No, I had never abandoned or abused my children.
I was always physically present.
But still — I carried my own guilt.
Guilt for the years I spent chasing stability,
for the missed recitals, the nights buried in textbooks, the weekends lost to work or study.
Guilt for choosing the hard road later in life
because I wasn't strong enough to finish what I started when I was young.
And those choices —
they cost me time.
They cost my family precious moments that no degree could ever replace.
So when Felix and my wife finally found their rhythm —

after years of silence and pain —
I celebrated with them.
Because I knew how rare it was for a daughter to get her father back.
And I knew how beautiful it was to witness love rebuilt from ashes.
He was a joyful grandfather —
full of hugs, full of laughter, full of cheesy dad jokes we both cracked up over.
My wife used to roll her eyes and say,
"Oh my God... I married my dad."
Now... he was gone.
And though we tried to focus on survival,
on hope, on homecoming —
His absence echoed in every corner of the room.
So yes — we celebrated.
We celebrated life.
We celebrated my return.
We celebrated a second chance.
But we also mourned.
Mourned the loss of a good man who didn't get his full redemption arc.
A grandfather who left too soon.
A father who had just begun to make things right.
A fellow dad-joke warrior and, in the end, a friend.
Never forgotten.
Always in our hearts.
Rest in peace, Felix Escoto Sr.
To my daughters...
If you read this someday, I want you to know—I'm sorry.
I'm sorry that I've been absent so often.

CHAPTER XIII: REQUIEM FOR THE LIVING

I'm sorry that you've had to carry the weight of the consequences of mistakes I made as a young man.

I've been working so hard because I just want this part of our lives—the struggle—to be over.

I want to reach the day where I can sit with you, laugh with you, share moments with you without being interrupted by "responsibilities" that mean nothing compared to time with you.

You are my greatest accomplishments.

My most treasured gifts.

There is nothing I have—nothing I will ever have—that could measure up to the place you hold in my heart.

I want to give you everything.

Everything you need.

Everything I can offer.

And when I'm old and grey, I want to still be there—no hesitation, no delay—to help you in any way I can.

Because loving you is not a task…

It's my honor.

Chapter XIV: The Shift with Felix

I started dating his mother when he was about seven years old. By the time he was nine, we were married. He was the ring bearer at our wedding, using an all-white Yankees cap as the cradle for the rings. His consistent invitations to "come over and play cars" were how his mother and I began our love story.

At the time, I was the guitarist in my church, Iglesia Cristiana Emanuel, on 156 Wilson Avenue in Bushwick, Brooklyn—a place I had called home since 1989, when my mother came to know Christ through my grandmother, Reina Sánchez.

Mi abuela was one of the pillars of our church community. Bold, consistent, and righteous, she was relentless in prayer. She prayed for her children, their spouses, her grandchildren, our neighborhood—even the drug addicts on the corner. If she met you, she was going to tell you about Jesus. And because of her faithfulness, generations were changed. My mother deepened her relationship with Christ because of her. I came to faith because of my mother and my children know the Lord because of my wife and I.

I remember the nights my mom would read scripture and pray with us. I treasure those memories. And it's something I try to do with my own children now. My hope is to leave the same legacy that was passed on to me—a legacy of faith, love,

CHAPTER XIV: THE SHIFT WITH FELIX

and consistency. My faith in Christ has carried me through the darkest valleys, including this one. Because He was "a very present help in trouble" (Psalm 46) and I believe He'll be just as real and present in my children's lives if they choose Him.

And to whomever is reading this, I don't know where you are in your journey, but I want you to know this: there is a God who loves you. He cares for you. He wants you to live and live abundantly. He offers peace beyond understanding—and if you're ready, you can invite Him into your life right now.

If you want to make a confession of faith, pray this with me:

"Jesus, I believe you are the Son of the one true God. You came to the world to be the sacrifice for my sins and the sins of all the world. I believe that you died and rose again on the third day, and because of your sacrifice, I am made new. I am now a son/daughter of the Father. Thank you for the gift of salvation. I surrender my heart to you. This I pray in Jesus' name, Amen."

If you prayed that prayer, find a church near you that teaches the Word of God. Surround yourself with other believers who will walk with you. And be kind to yourself—God doesn't require perfection. He calls us to excellence. There's a difference. Anyone who tries to sell you perfection, run, don't walk, run away from them because that's not the heart of God for any of us.

Welcome to the family. God bless you.

Now... back to my story.

From an early age, Felix had to contend with a lot of inconsistencies in his life. A father who wasn't truly present the way a father should be. Power struggles and differences in parenting between his mother, his grandmother, and his uncle— also named Felix—whom he affectionately called "papatío" (uncle-father).

They all loved Felix dearly and had the best of intentions, but like all of us, they weren't perfect. Their efforts often collided, creating tension and conflict in the home. Felix was strong-willed, with a unique way of thinking and doing things that set him apart. As a child, that inquisitive nature, coupled with his curt approach, was often mistaken for disrespect—but looking back, I don't think he was always trying to be disrespectful. He just didn't know how to ask the difficult questions or approach difficult topics that were storming in his young mind.

In Latino culture, questioning an adult is often seen as insolence. In my mother's time, children weren't even allowed to speak in the presence of adults. If they did, they got whacked—and that's putting it lightly. By the time Felix was growing up in the late 90s and early 2000s, not much had changed.

But Felix was always ahead of his time. I saw that early on. When he was around 10 or 11, he asked to speak with me. "Yo Ant," he said, "can I talk to you?"

"Yeah, son. Absolutely," I replied.

He sat me down in his room and apologized for giving me a hard time about the rules I was trying to establish in the home. "Before you got here," he said, "I did whatever I wanted. My mom gave me whatever I wanted. I never had someone tell me what needed to be done."

Those may not have been his exact words, but the heart behind them was clear. Even at that age, he could articulate what he was feeling, admit when he was wrong, and express what he wanted. Grown men struggle to do that.

That cycle—contention and reconciliation—would continue throughout his adolescence and even into adulthood. We've faced some dark and difficult times in our relationship as

CHAPTER XIV: THE SHIFT WITH FELIX

father and son. Many people would say your "step-son" and, semantically, they were right but, this was not an issue of semantics. For me, words have weight. The words we use to express ourselves have power and impact and in my heart, the message was always the same, this young man is my son and I had committed the paternal part of my heart to him regardless of what the world wanted to say on the matter.

I never referred to Felix as my "stepson." Even before his mother and I were married, I asked her if she wanted me to raise Felix as my own. She said yes. And from that moment, he was my son—in heart, in mind, and in commitment.

I may not always agree with his choices, but I made a vow to him (within myself) before I vowed to be his mother's husband.

And just like my heavenly Father never gives up on me, I won't give up on Felix.

(I pray for you every day, son.

And I'm believing in God for your life— That it will be aligned with His perfect will.)

I never took the role of absolute ruler. I believe in conversations with my kids. In journeying together toward wisdom. In encouraging them to think deeply and seek truth patiently. That's why the Bible teaches us to be "quick to hear, slow to speak, slow to anger."

As Felix got older, his outbursts became more aggressive— and I met his fire with fire. I should have de-escalated more often. But like everyone else, I'm not perfect. I made mistakes. A lot of them.

Over time, I shifted into more of an advisor. Once your kids are adults, you don't tell them what to do—you offer perspective. You guide. And you hope they make wise choices.

Felix was hungry for success. He wanted to be rich. He read

a lot about financial literacy. and once his mind was set, he stopped looking to me for advice because the truth was, I was never good at managing money or building wealth. He was on his own path.

We were struggling financially, and I told him that we needed help. In my house, if you're not in school, you get a job. You contribute until you're ready to move out. We helped him get a car because he said he wanted to drive for Uber. That didn't happen. Eventually, the car was repossessed. I had co-signed. My credit took the hit. It created a lot of tension between us. But we worked through it. We reconciled.

And then... I got sick.

On the day I was taken to the hospital, before I was intubated, all that tension still lingered. But after I returned, Felix asked to speak with me again—just like he had when he was ten. He said he was glad I made it back because he didn't want the way I left—sick and weak—to be the last time he saw me.

He had done a lot of soul-searching while I was in that coma. He stepped up. He was there for his mother. For his sisters. He held down the crib when I couldn't. He answered the call that every father hopes their son will one day answer.

For that, I am forever grateful.

Thank you, Felix, for being the guardian of our home when I couldn't be.

I love you, son.

We're both still a work in progress. No man's story is over until he's dead and buried. But I hope we both continue to be men who love God and love our families.

Felix is now married. He's a partner in an auto body shop in Queens. I'm proud of his free spirit and, even envy sometimes, his courage to take chances and bet on himself. Proud that he

CHAPTER XIV: THE SHIFT WITH FELIX

knows what he wants. My prayer is that he learns to balance his ambitions with the needs of those around him. If he finds that balance, I believe everything he wants will be within reach.

Chapter XV: From Wreckage to Work

It got to the point where my wife would no longer look at me with eyes of love or want. Her gaze was full of hurt. Disgust. Not because of how I looked—but because of what we had become. One day, she told me she didn't know if she loved me anymore. That I had never given her her rightful place as my wife. That I hadn't protected her from the criticism of others.

I was blindsided.

I didn't understand. I never saw those comments as direct attacks. They felt like passing jabs. But for her, they were paper cuts that never healed. And my silence—my failure to stand up—became betrayal.

She had hoarded years of pain. Years of resentment. And by the time it all came spilling out, it had attached itself to me.

I felt the earth fall out from beneath me. I was free falling into a void.

She was the love of my life. I had never loved anyone the way I loved her. And suddenly, she was gone.

That was one of the darkest periods of my life. I wrote this poem during that time:

CHAPTER XV: FROM WRECKAGE TO WORK

Space

by Anthony Sánchez
I wish I knew what it felt like
To not need love
To not ache from the absence of her warmth
To not hunger for the surge she causes within me
To not desire her embrace and be fed by the lips that speak my name
To not want to hear my name on her lips and feel the power of her unsolicited affirmations.
I am so entranced by her beauty, so intoxicated by her breasts.
Space is my enemy but now, he is her closest friend
She takes counsel from him and is comforted by him.
I hate the man... and if he were manifested,
I'd eliminate his existence so that we could be together... but...
for now,
Space is necessary.
She needs him— I need her but she needs Space.
It appears that the thing I hate the most, is what I'll need to trust to bring her back to me...
Space... my worst enemy has become my trusted ally
in the battle for the heart of my beloved.

That poem came from the raw center of my pain. And eventually, that pain overflowed into every room of our home. We couldn't keep pretending. Something had to give.

Eventually, I moved out. Things were too toxic for either of us to keep living under the same roof.

Returning to my mother's home was humbling. I felt like a failure. I had built my own family. I had made a vow. I had proposed in my heart to love one woman for the rest of my life—and I had never broken that vow. I never cheated. Never even looked elsewhere.

But I was broken. And waking up in my childhood home was a constant reminder of how far I had fallen.

I did things I'm not proud of. Things I won't detail here. Not illegal, not malicious—but they violated my own values. My walk with God suffered. My identity suffered.

What saved me was the work.

Oddly enough, in the middle of my wreckage, people still saw me as whole.

Being a teacher. A coach. A mentor.

My school community still looked to me. My students still needed me. Whether it was teaching Spanish, culinary skills, or coaching basketball—they were relying on me to show up. And to do that, I had to rebuild.

I had to take a long, painful look in the mirror.

Rebuild my spirit.

Rebuild my habits.

Rebuild my purpose.

Accept what I had done.

Own what I had failed to do.

Repent.

Heal.

And start walking in grace again.

Abounding Grace Ministries—my church family—became a lifeline. My pastor. My friends, Eli and Courtney, you guys were fresh water to me during some of the most difficult moments in this whole ordeal. The music we made together, the conversations, the encouragement, and the hard truths you were always willing to deliver in such gracious and loving ways

CHAPTER XV: FROM WRECKAGE TO WORK

were all an elixir to my soul. I love you both. The worship. The Word. The prayers. All of it slowly stitched me back together. Their love for me and my wife individually helped us both soften. Eventually... We found our way back to each other.

And one moment that helped begin that journey back happened about a year after my COVID recovery. I was in excruciating pain and rushed to the hospital again. This time—for emergency gallbladder surgery. I was worn down. Physically exhausted. Vulnerable. And in that place of fragility, she came to me. She showed up with tenderness I hadn't felt in a long time. She helped care for me. She helped me recover. And not just physically. That moment—oddly enough—marked the beginning of our healing. It was as if God knew I needed to be brought low again, not as punishment, but as a reintroduction. A reminder that love shows up when things fall apart. And as I grew in my faith again, I started growing in wisdom, too.

I'm finally learning what I wish I had known years ago. How to manage money. The difference between a liability and an asset. That being from Bushwick is no excuse for financial ignorance. To all my people who grew up in communities like mine, our beginnings are not a justification for continuing in the ignorance we may or may not have been raised in. We should strive for more, fight for more, and push the limits of what we think we can do. That's what I have been doing and it's what I will continue to do until I've completely destroyed that voice inside my head that says "you can't because...(insert excuse here). I refuse to allow anyone, not even myself, to get in the way of the growth and success that God has already planned for me.

Fortunately, I have so many great people in my life who are gifted and successful. My Uncle Eric, an extremely successful professional in his field, has been helping me build a plan to achieve a more financially stable situation, enabling me to have a greater impact. I've made mistakes, gotten us into debt—but I'm working to correct it. That's what we all need to do. As a people, we need to humble ourselves and learn to ask for help when we don't know something. That's not a sign of weakness y'all. That shows great strength. In this season of my life, I will no longer remain in ignorance, because my legacy matters. I want the work I do now—not just to rebuild my own life—but to set up something better for those I love. So when the day comes for me to leave this earth, my seed will continue to show love and impact the communities they live in. Whether it's in Bushwick or another part of this beautiful planet. This is the legacy I'm leaving.

THE END

Epilogue

Still Becoming

The journey didn't end when I walked out of the hospital in April 2020. In fact, in many ways, it was just beginning.

What most people didn't know was that while I was in a coma, catheters had been placed in both ends of me. The one in my colon caused a small, undetectable hole—what doctors later identified as a fistula. Because of that tiny breach, fecal matter would slowly seep into the surrounding soft tissue, causing recurrent infections and abscesses to form.

A few months after I left the hospital, I began developing painful abscesses near my upper right glute. Sometimes they were small. At other times, the inflammation would become so severe that the area turned purple, swollen, and rock-hard. The pain made simple things—walking, sitting, even driving—nearly impossible.

I lived with this pain—off and on—for over three years. It affected everything: driving, coaching, teaching, even walking. I remember trying to coach a middle school baseball game while barely able to stand. I did what I could to push through, but the pain was always there, lurking beneath the surface. Sometimes the abscesses would rupture on their own. Other times, I had to go to the ER to have them drained surgically.

I missed work. I missed family events, and in January 2024, I missed something that still breaks my heart to this day—my good friend and brother Osh's funeral. While the whole neighborhood came together to honor his life, I was in the hospital again, fighting off another infection that nearly made me septic.

If you're not from Eldert Street, you might not understand what Osh meant to us. He was the heart of our block—the one who organized our annual block parties, made sure every kid got ice cream, and created an atmosphere where love and community could thrive. He made everyone feel welcome, no matter where they came from. He was family. Today, our brother James "Pop" Willis and the rest of the Long family continue that tradition, keeping Osh's legacy alive the best way we know how—by showing up for our people.

But here's the beautiful part: after years of suffering in silence, I found a surgeon named Dr. Patricia Sylla from Mount Sinai who, in her words, was able to "fix my butt." And let me tell you—she did. I've been abscess-free since April 2025, and I can finally say I'm healing for real.

What I've learned through all of this is simple but unshakable: life's trials don't stop, but we get to decide how we respond. We don't have to be defined by our pain, our losses, or even our scars. We can grow. We can move forward. We can still

EPILOGUE

become.

That's where I'm headed next.

I'm already outlining my second book—this one for educators. It's about the power of connection in the classroom and the heart behind my teaching philosophy: *connect before you correct.* Because kids don't learn from people they don't trust. And trust is built when we choose to see, hear, and love them first.

I've still got work to do. But I'm here. I'm alive. And I'm still grindin'.

About the Author

Anthony Sánchez is a husband and father, an educator, audio engineer, worship leader, die-hard Knicks fan, and proud Dominican son of Brooklyn, New York. After surviving a near-death experience during the COVID-19 pandemic, he found a renewed sense of purpose in his family, faith, and community. He now teaches middle school Spanish, mentors young musicians, coaches basketball and baseball, and leads worship at his home church in the Lower East Side.

Also known by his artist name Tony Max, Anthony is a recording artist whose music reflects the same resilience, faith, and raw honesty explored in this memoir. His album Love Yourself was born out of the same recovery that inspired this book—especially the track "Edge of My Heart," which was written after one of the vivid dreams he experienced while in a coma. Can you guess which dream inspired it? Come to a book signing and ask him yourself. You can stream the album